Sculpture: form and method

Architectural Association

Cover
St Michael, painted woodcarving p
Collection Blair Hughes-Stanton

Page 2
The Assumption of the Virgin, Rohr  ɔrks

Sculpture: form and method
Bernard Myers

Studio Vista: London
Reinhold Publishing Corporation: New York

A Studio Vista/Reinhold Art Paperback
Edited by John Lewis
© Bernard Myers 1965
Published in London by Studio Vista Limited
Blue Star House, Highgate Hill, London N19
and in New York by Reinhold Publishing Corporation
430 Park Avenue, New York
Library of Congress catalog card number 65–24056
Set in 9/12 Univers Medium 689
Printed in the Netherlands
by N.V. Drukkerij Koch & Knuttel, Gouda

Contents

ACKNOWLEDGEMENTS

To Graham Clarke for finding the illustrations. The author's knowledge
of sculptors' techniques is founded on the lectures and conversation
of the late Karel Vogel.

SCULPTURE

Introduction

Column figures from Royal
Portal, 12th century
Notre Dame Cathedral, Chartres
photo: Giraudon

There is an immediate inherent difficulty to be faced in any book
about sculpture. It is that of adequately reproducing the works
discussed. The illustrations in guides and catalogues to paintings
and drawings have a twofold effect: that of reminding us of
work that we have seen, and of familiarising us with works which
we have not seen, so that if and when we ever do come face to
face with them we are already familiar with them to a certain
extent and know what to look for. There is generally something
more than we bargained for in the original work itself, and this
makes the pursuit of pictures very exciting and also is a timely
reminder that a reproduction is never a substitute for the real
thing, and should not be used as such.

Within reasonable limits the kind of reproduction does not matter
greatly. A black and white reproduction can be of more use than
a coloured one for certain purposes, and engraved reproductions
originally made for picture-books have come to be regarded as
minor works of art in their own right.

In the field of sculpture, however, it is not only the immediate
disparity between the three-dimensional sculpture and a two-
dimensional picture that is the stumbling block. Good stereoscopic
photographs could give us the illusion of the extra dimension
and would still be quite inadequate. For stereoscopic pictures
must be taken from one viewpoint, and even a series of stereoscopic views could not give one any hint of the essence of
experiencing sculpture as art, which is the movement of the
spectator across or round the work. As we walk about sculpture
the changes are infinitely small, and one of the major qualities
of sculpture lies in the sculptor's conscious or unconscious use of
parallax; that is to say, the apparent relative movement of forms
close to us against those that are farther away.

When looking at sculpture we can walk up to it, back away,
walk round it, retrace our steps, stoop for a low viewpoint, move
in under it or to a distance to perceive the whole as we wish, on
the spur of the moment. Not even a three-dimensional film of
sculpture could give us this experience.

If the number of books on fine art is any guide, there are more people now interested in looking at pictures than at any time before. Long before the tourist finds himself in one of the great national galleries of the world, he has some sort of acquaintance with the pictures he is going to see. There is no such ready-made audience for sculpture. Nor is it usually seen at its best in museum settings. A picture frame can enclose us in a world of its own, making us temporarily forget the most uncomfortable or distracting surroundings; rather like reading a book in a crowded train where the white margin cuts us off completely from our jostling neighbours. Sculpture must be seen against its surroundings. It cannot be framed except by them. Sculpture is not an easy art to appreciate, and the difficulty is often increased by bad siting.

A short handbook such as this is not the proper place for discussion of the difficulties of siting or the right use of sculpture, which are properly architectural problems. What I wish to do here is to point out some of these problems which together at the present time tend to make sculpture a relatively neglected art.

Chapter 1 The origins

Man could draw before he could write, perhaps almost before he could speak, and certainly before language had achieved any formal structure. The growth of set forms of language and the development of graphic signs bring with them abstraction, for this is what they themselves essentially are.

The work of psychologists and anthropologists and, above all the advantage of hind-sight has helped us to accept the unexpected realism of Palaeolithic cave-art. Indeed, if people incapable of abstraction to any great degree produce works of art, then we should expect this work to be realistic.

These people had a struggle to exist at all without any technological shield between them and their environment, and had to rely on food-finding and hunting with all the attending accidents instead of food-growing and manufactures which are predictable. The extraordinary thing is that they found both time and energy not only to produce painting and sculpture but also jewelry and

Fragment of spear thrower
from La Madeleine, France
Musée des Antiquités Nationales

trinkets of sorts, bangles and bracelets, necklaces of fish vertebrae as delicately graded as a string of pearls.

Cave painting evinces bravura as well as an eye for realism. Again we should expect people with highly developed physical reactions to put a quality of gesture into this work. However, on closer examination, the brush stroke which flows with such fluid grace has been preceded by an engraved line, and one cannot run a graving tool through hard rock in a single spontaneous stroke such as one might make with a brush. Thus this apparently free and spontaneous gesture may in fact be most carefully calculated. In the caves the engraver-painters were working on a virtually unlimited surface. The sculptor proper had to convert his piece of stone, ivory or bone into his three dimensional image, and achieved his realism in spite of the restrictions of surface limitations and a more intractable medium.

The purpose of sculpture may have been quite different from that of the cave painting too. The paintings were part of magic rites as preparation for hunting. The sculptures may have been carried as magic charms to work in the hunting expedition itself, or to protect the owner, but much of the engraving on tools must have served secondary purposes, those of pure pride in tool and weapon making, and then as marks of ownership and recognition, the equivalent of initials or armorial bearings.

The Paleolithic sculptor worked on bone and ivory with stone tools as beautiful and precise as his carvings. He probably also worked in more perishable materials, wood and clay. As with the cave paintings only those works have survived which were accidentally sealed up in caves. There must have been many more paintings on exposed rock shelters and cliff faces which have perished, and so it must have been with clay and wood statuettes at whose existence in quantity we can only guess. The fragment of a spear thrower from La Madeleine in France has all the qualities of fine sculpture. The essence of a work of art lies not in imitation but analogy. The spear thrower is primarily carved to give greater handgrip. The carving is reminiscent of flight feathers or fish fins, arranged precisely and alternately down each side of the bone. Consciously or unconsciously, they are strongly associated with flight and speed. Although on a small scale, the arrangement is architectural and monumental before these qualities existed as such. Here is something more than the perfunctory engraving on an antler surface. There is a certain kind of immortality in works of art. When we look at them we are looking over the artist's shoulder while he is at work, although he lived 30,000 years ago or more.

There is an important series of female statuettes carved in mammoth-tusk ivory found all over Europe. These date from the Gravettian period (50,000 years ago, named after the La Gravette rock shelter in the Dordogne). All have highly developed female characteristics with greatly exaggerated buttocks. This may not be so stylised, for the Bush women of southern Africa show the same steatopygical development which would be thought to be caricatured if the Bush people were not still in existence. There may have been strong physical resemblances between Paleolithic and Bush people.

These statuettes have been found at Willendorf, near Vienna, at Menton in the French Riviera and Vestonice in Moravia. They may have been cult objects, early statuettes of a Mother Goddess, forerunners of Aphrodite, Venus or Astarte.

The great Ice Age brought the Old Stone Age to an end. The succeeding New Stone Age society shows the change from one based on hunting to one based on herding and early agriculture. Here rudimentary counting and measuring must have been necessary, and man had to develop his powers of abstraction. This development is evident in the arts of the New Stone Age which become abstracted and symbolic. Actual animals and people become patterned forms. Man invented the potter's wheel and became a technologist. The statuettes become patterned slabs, a circle is a head, two more are breasts, and the pubic region a simple cross or Y. In the West the whole development from Stone Age to Bronze Age is a mystery, but the late Stone Age sculptures are the direct ancestors of the incised menhir or standing stones of Brittany. These, like the ritual circle at Stonehenge, may be much later than hitherto supposed, even contemporary with early Greece. Elsewhere in Africa, America and Australia Stone Age cultures have lasted to the present day.

There may be said to be an unbroken line of descent from the Stone Age work of Africa to that of Ancient Egypt. The earlier Egyptian wall decorations show the same incised line enclosing painted forms, and there is no strong dividing line between carved relief and mural painting. These early reliefs are technically sculpture since they are carved, but cannot be considered in the same way as the later Greek and Roman sculpture reliefs. They are inextricably part of a system closer to incised lettering and symbols, which form an equal part of the reliefs. These were not considered as works of art but as message-bearing tablets. They are found in buried tombs, perhaps because the above-ground buildings of the earlier dynasties have mostly perished, but it must be emphasised that all Egyptian art, nearly 5,000 years of it, has a strong funereal flavour. The next world was as real as this to the Egyptians, and much more important, for this was temporary, the next eternal. The tomb friezes, painted or carved, told those in the next world what sort of person their occupant was in this (serving as a kind of personal file), and also gave the occupant valuable instructions on what to do on arrival. As Egyptian society became more settled and the system of laws grew, so this state of affairs was mirrored in the elaborate bureaucracy of the next world depicted. The picture did not change in concept but became more and more complicated.

Something of this may be seen in the Egyptian pyramid. Essentially it is a heap of stones over a grave. Bodies could not be buried in the hard shale and clay of the Eastern desert, and had to be protected from jackals and vultures by a cairn of rocks piled over a shallow trench. The difference between the simple cairn and elaborate pyramid is one of scale, technological development and social organisation; the idea remains the same.

So it is with Egyptian sculpture. The idea, once it had evolved, remained the same for 5,000 years. There are changes, but these are of scale and technique. There are cycles of growth and decay which enable the egyptologist to identify otherwise undated works. Copies of copies lead to certain degenerations of form. Eventually this decline becomes such that an effort of rediscovery has to be made, and once more technical control of form

Priest conducting opening of the mouth ceremony, (detail), Egyptian stone relief, c. 1400 B.C.
By permission of the Trustees, British Museum, London

grows in an heroic phase until a peak is reached, and once more it declines into copies of copies.

The set forms of Egyptian sculpture seem to have been finally arrived at simultaneously with those of the hieroglyphics, the Egyptian pictorial alphabet.

These sculptural forms are almost picture-writing in themselves. The human figure is compounded of a system of set symbols for every part of the body. These are assembled in what seems to us to be a contradictory manner. The head is carved in profile, but the eye is superimposed as seen full face. The shoulders and upper torso are also full view, but the arms, hips and legs are drawn as from the side. This is the carving of a man, yet not of a man. It is like an architect's drawing of a house, or an engineer's blueprint of an article. All the parts are there, it is perfectly recognisable, yet it is not the man nor the object as we see it.

This is no naïve assemblage of typical views. It used to be held

Two heads found by the British expedition in the palace of the Oba of Benin, bronze, both 8.25 ins
British Museum and Schnell Collection *Photo: William Fagg*

13

that the Egyptians put together a profile head and a frontal ey
because these are the easiest views to draw or carve, or becaus
they could not see three-dimensional relationships, but this i
not so, as we can see from their perfectly rational three-dimensiona
sculpture.

Perhaps the clue lies here. The comparison of an Egyptian relie
figure with a blueprint or working drawing for a figure is apt, fo
in their sculpture the Egyptians used the same series of elevation
or views that an engineer uses today in a working drawing.

In making a statue, a solid block of wood or stone was carefull
prepared and reasonably well finished by masons as a rectangula
prism stood on end. Then a series of views of the figure wer
carefully drawn on the four sides of the solid, the front, bac
and two side elevations. The side elevations were almost alway
of a figure with one leg advanced, as in the reliefs.

These elevations were enlarged by squaring up from maste
drawings on papyrus. These drawings were as set as an alphabe
Each drawing in the master book was covered with a grid c
squares. Co-ordinate points could be taken from these rectangula
grids and enlarged to any size. The proportions were thus alway
constant, whether the finished work was a smaller than life-siz
statuette or a colossal figure cut into a cliff face. These rules fo
artists were obeyed as automatically as any social rule may be toda
The next step in carving was to cut away superfluous stone t
join the elevations together. The figure at this stage would loo
rather like a nineteenth-century, slab-sided, wooden toy figur
The corners were then rounded off and the figure gradually too
its final shape. The stone was chipped away in all-over layer
as if being peeled to reveal the figure inside. Finally, the maste
carver would chisel the details of features and drapery, and th
figure would be finished again by assistants. A wooden figur
would be given a thin coat of bitumen or plaster; painted an
perhaps gilded ; a stone figure would be polished and burnishe
to a mirror finish.

The sculptors worked in teams organised on a basis of divisio
of labour for each operation, in exactly the same way as a moder
factory mass-production line. The tools were stone, bronze an
later iron.

Within this rigid framework a degree of variation was possibl
Figures of gods and goddesses were carved entirely to a formul

but individual figures of Pharaohs, priests and important laymen are recognisable portraits. As long as the method, the pose, the unemotional mask-like expression and the canon of proportion were observed, the figure could be thin or fat, long or short nosed and so on. These details would be taken from life. Plaster casts of faces have been excavated on the site of sculptors' workshops, and they may have taken their portraits from these. It is a mistake to attribute modern ideas of freedom to the artists of ancient Egypt and pity them for lack of opportunity to express themselves. They simply would not have understood what such terms meant. Making works of art was a social-religious business with the same laws as those of a science such as astronomy. Once one has penetrated the rather formidable barrier of apparent expressionless sameness that confronts one in museum Egyptian departments, one can find a great deal of superb statuary of kings and queens, gods, men and animals. The technical finish has never been surpassed. Immaculate surfaces and fineness of line, the flow of three-dimensional curved planes are all equal to that of today's aeronautical engineers.

The Egyptians perpetuated the Stone Age into historical times. They carved great, stone, tank-like tombs from solid blocks of the hardest stone, with knife-edge corners and inner mirror-flat planes meeting at exact right angles, and turned bowls, vases and lamps from equally hard stone. Their technology was the foundation of Greek culture, and their form lasted into Graeco-Roman times without being affected by them. After such an unbroken tradition one would expect to find surviving traces much later, and indeed one does in the highly developed portrait-sculpture of west Africa.

Chapter 3 Egypt and Assyria

There are strong resemblances and equally strong differences between Egyptian works of art and those of the parallel civilisations of the great crescent from Anatolia and Persia in the north, down the Tigris and Euphrates valleys to the Persian Gulf in the south. These echo the similarities and differences of these neighbour societies.

Egyptian conservatism was the result of thousands of years of un challenged material security. Egypt was physically protected by the narrow isthmus in the north and east, and by mountains and deserts in the south and west. Her arable land was renewed with rich deposits from the Nile every year. The black mud and favour able climate gave two annual crops for very little manual work. Consequently there was an abundance of cheap food and free man-power for most of the year, enabling large-scale state monu ments to be built by a system of conscripted labour.

The society was based on land tenure and agriculture, with the king as supreme landlord. Inheritance was clearly defined and extended to posts in the army and civil service, which included the official artists. It is clear from Egyptian statuary and reliefs that the main clothing was of linen, a vegetable fibre grown as a crop. The Assyrian figures wore woollen garments decorated with heavy tassels. Their society was based on herding sheep, goats, camel and cattle. Their cities were on exposed sites in great plains, and were fortified centres where the wealthy semi-nomadic grazier marketed their wool, hides and livestock. They imported grain from Egypt and Central Asia, and the king's wealth was based on import export taxes and tariffs. The rich cities invited attack from neigh bours, and the great mounds, all that are left of them today, show evidence of many consecutive cities rebuilt and destroyed again on the same site. Stone was scarce and the earth of the plains, as burnt or sun-dried brick, was the chief building material.

Assyrian society was more nervous and unstable than that of the Egyptians. Fortunes could be made and lost by gráziers and mer chants, and kings could be enslaved by rivals and their cities and palaces destroyed overnight.

The great brick palaces and temples were decorated with relief panels in carved brick and stone, the latter generally a soft lime stone marble rather than the iron hard granites and basalts favoured in Egypt. The same laws of frontality are observed, and their pursuance to a logical conclusion of an extreme degree sometimes produced what appear in modern eyes to be illogical results.

The main staircase entrance to the king's palace at Khorsabad was guarded by seraphs. These guardian angels portray in literal symbols the attributes of those other-worldly beings. They have the sagacity of a man, the strength of a bull and the speed of an eagle – a man's head, a bull's body and an eagle's wings. Similar seraphs formed the throne of King Solomon. The seraph is carved with skill, striking that balance between the familiar recognition of features, hair, feathers and their geometrization into formal patterns that remove them from this world to an unchanging, timeless eternity. The general appearance of the man-headed bull is forbidding, but then that was as it should be.

The one apparent flaw in the sculpture is that the creature has five legs when seen in threequarter view. If the sculptor was alive and able to answer his critics, he would probably say that he knew perfectly well that no bull has five legs, but there was no other way of carving it. Convention demanded that in the side view it should be shown in mid stride like any other figure. Thus all four legs may be seen. From the front, the stone could not be undercut to the extent necessary for the back slanting foreleg to connect with the shallow relief of the side. The forelegs, therefore, had to be carved side by side, at attention so to speak. The answer is thus that the bull only *appears* to have five legs, and an Assyrian contemporary who interpreted a symbolic work of art with literal realism would have been considered a naïve ignoramus.

This is well in keeping with other conventions of the time. Objects are placed one above the other on the picture plane of a relief, when they are actually one behind the other. Size is not governed by an idea of space in which objects appear to diminish with distance, but by a table of hieratic importance. Men are more important than trees and buildings, and are therefore carved larger. Men are more important than women, and are carved larger again. Free men are more important than slaves or prisoners, and the king most important of all.

Nevertheless the strict conventions do not obscure an extremely well developed sense of analytical vision for observed detail. In the huge friezes from Khorsabad we have as accurate a record of warfare of the time as any modern newsreel might give. Armoured

Assur-Bhani-Pal hunting a lion, Assyrian stone relief
By permission of the Trustees, British Museum, London

vehicles, battering rams and siege towers could be reconstructed from the details given. Men are shown crossing rivers on inflated skins for a surprise attack, chariots manned by archers manoeuvre in open warfare.

Because of the armed-frontier life of the region, the carvings are more active and more savage than those of Egypt, and more nervous and fluid in line. Perhaps the finest of all Assyrian sculptures is the relief of the lion hunt of Assur-Bhani-Pal. The lion hunt was staged in the arena like a bullfight, and the king led the performance. The wounded lions and lioness are anatomically perfect. Without any sentimental pity for animals the sculptor expresses all the agony of their death throws as they drag themselves about on paralysed limbs. At the same time muscles and sinews, hair and even flowing blood are controlled by a strict geometrization that keeps the whole scene firmly within the laid-down hieratic convention.

The Greeks took over all their stone-working technology from the Egyptians and the contemporary civilisations of Asia Minor. Their previous buildings and sculptures had been worked in timber, brick and terra-cotta. The Spartans were still building mainly in brick and timber, and decorating these buildings with terra-cotta sculpture, during the final civil war that ended in ruin for both Athens and Sparta and finished the flowering of an independent Greek culture. The Greeks had settled in a peninsular which was comparatively barren. Hard living conditions forced them to think and to economise. They had to take to the sea, and were pirates as much as merchants. They lived in small communities where the individual bore a great deal of responsibility. They were both original and eclectic, seizing on anything that came to hand by way of techniques, ideas and materials, and putting them to their own peculiar use. Their restlessness eventually led to their own self-destruction. Some of the earliest surviving statuary shows the combination of wood working with the new stone carving. The figures, *kore* or girls bearing votive offerings, are columnar, as if carved from a round tree trunk. The figure from the waist down is almost completely cylindrical, and the gracefully pleated skirt reminds one of a fluted column. The right arm held a votive offering, perhaps an apple or pomegranate, many-seeded emblems of fertility. This arm, at right angles to the vertical axis of the body, was carved separately and pegged into its socket with a carpenter's tongued joint as if in a wooden statue. The weakest part of the statue, this joint, was bound to fail when the statues were overthrown from whatever cause, and the *kore* are found with an empty socket at the elbow. Contemporary with these *kore* are *kouros*, boys. These young men obey the Egyptian laws of frontality, taken over by the Greeks together with the techniques. They stand in mid stride, one leg advanced, arms rigidly at their sides, gazing straight ahead. These archaic figures are crude and provincial by comparison with their Egyptian models, already the result of two thousand years or more of continuous civilisation. They have neither the realism of Egyptian portraiture nor the crisp accuracy of the Egyptian abstract ideal. But even in their earliest stages they are more human. They are not so expressionless, outside the world of space and time. A quiet smile plays about the features, placid and enigmatic, calm and relaxed.

Kore girl bearing votive offering, c. 510
Athens, National Museum *Photo: Hannibal, Athens*

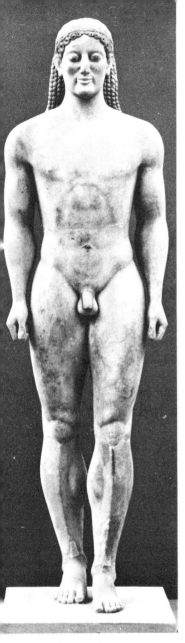

Kouros 'Croesus' from Anavysos,
Attica, 550–525
Athens, National Museum

This is not the only difference. The Egyptians evolved their techniques to deal with very hard stones, granites and basalts. With only stone or, later, bronze tools to work with, they could not chisel away great masses of stone, but had to pound and splinter it and later polish it to shape. The Greeks carved in marble, crystalline but softer, and consequently it was concussed and stunned by the hammering. Bruised to a depth of about three-eighths of an inch, the marble lost its translucency and remained slightly pitted all over, incapable of taking a high polish like the glass-hard basalt. Most of the Greek statues in our museums thus look to have been carved in a more opaque stone than marble. This pearly quality of pitting enables the sculpture to take light and shade on form without any disturbing highlights and reflections. It has an almost skin-like porous quality. It must be remembered that Greek sculptures, like the marble buildings, were often brightly coloured. The texture enabled the wax emulsion paint or a plaster skin to key into the stone surface.

The Greek sculptor worked very like his Egyptian counterpart. A block of stone was selected and trimmed to size. The elevations were outlined on the faces of the block and the stone cut down to the outline. If the work was large, this would be done at the quarry itself to save the effort and expense of transporting superfluous stone. The pointed tool was used as a punch rather than a chisel. Multiple pointed tools were also used as punches, not as claw chisels. In the early stages the stone was smashed away. At each successive stage the handling of the punch became more delicate. The figure was in effect revealed by the removing of concentric layers of stone, as if peeling an onion. Finally, a sharp pointed, triangular or edged mason's chisel was used to give a sharp edge to features such as eyelids or the outline of lips. Special round-nosed chisels were used to groove out drapery folds in the same manner as flutes were cut into columns.

The Egyptians used rubbing stones and grades of sand and pumice powder to give the finely polished finish to their work. The Greeks, perhaps for aesthetic reasons and almost certainly because of a different attitude towards time and labour, used metal rasps for the final finish. They also made use of drills, sometimes to drill a series of holes which could then be joined into a groove by a few blows from the mallet and punch, and often as a running drill. While being worked the drill was guided across the surface of the stone to

Horse and rider (unfinished) found at Sparta, stone
By permission of the Trustees, British Museum, London

cut a continuous channel, the same principle used in a modern milling or spindle machine.

From the beginning the Greeks used no canon law to regularise their sculpture once and for all. By a gradual process of sculptural evolution the frontal figure began to turn, to place his weight on one leg or the other, demanding counterpoise in the pose.

This may have originated from the art of casting in terra-cotta, which was practised from earliest times, but which of course was fragile and easily destroyed. Even if this growing flexibility did not originate in casting, it was certainly helped by it. The Greeks not only made small clay or wax figurines as models for large-scale carvings, they also made full size models for pedimental and other sculpture. These would have been too heavy to handle in solid clay and so were hollow cast in terra-cotta or plaster.

Much sculpture was also cast in bronze, of course. The technique used was the lost wax method. A wax figure was made and coated with a refractory slurry of terra-cotta or pottery clay. The whole was fired and the wax melted out, leaving a hollow mould for bronze. Sand moulds may also have been used, the molten metal forcing out the wax.

Unfortunately very few of these bronzes have survived. Later ages found them more important as sources of good metal than as works of art. We merely know of most of the bronzes through Roman marble copies which are shadows of the originals, not only because what is self-supporting in bronze needs supports in the shape of bracketed tree trunks and other clumsy devices in stone, but also because the copies themselves are debased to meet the emotional needs of a decadent patronage.

Among the best surviving bronzes is the magnificent charioteer from Delphi. The pose is straight, yet the linear quality of the fine bronze casting gives the charioteer a lithe look, more supple and elastic than many more violently posed pieces of sculpture. Detail was originally picked out in gold leaf, and the eyes were enamelled inlay. To match him are the famous bronze horses now crowning the façade of St Mark's in Venice. These are of a later date than the charioteer. They too were covered in gold leaf, and here too the bronze has a supple, elastic appearance.

Most classical Greek sculpture is now in the great museums of the world. Here we have constantly to remind ourselves of the civic settings for which the sculpture was intended. This is particularly true of sculpture produced as an integral part of architecture, such as the pedimental figures and the relief frieze from the Parthenon now in the British Museum in London. As we walk around the galleries we have to realise that much of the free standing pedimental figures would be hardly visible. This is true of much of Egyptian sculpture as well. Here carved friezes and figures com-

Charioteer from Delphi, c 470
Delphi Museum *Photo: Alison Frantz*

pletely hidden by ledges and parapets were finished to perfection out of a sense of abstract religious duty. The finishing of the backs of attached Greek sculpture has a rather different reason. As the choice of pose open to the sculptor developed away from frontality, the planes became more complex than those from the simple development of four elevations. The form became a series of three-dimensional continuous curves with no demarcation between front, back and side. Consequently the carver had to work all round a figure, no matter from which angle it was to be viewed. The part of the sculpture seen could not work unless continued right out of sight. The hidden parts of the piece, however, were not finished right up to the last stage of light chiselling and rubbing down, and consequently give us a true guide to the stages of finish in Greek carving.

Greek reliefs are more than the incised linear drawing of the Egyptians. The tools and carving techniques are the same as carving in the round, but the nearer surface forms are flattened, and it is the further forms that are undercut and rounded. This is in apparent contradiction to the common visual experience, where near objects have the greatest changes of form and the farther appear to flatten out. The effect of the Greek formula is to preserve the mural surface and keep the sculpture subordinate to an architectural scheme.

There are no such things as rules for producing works of art. Nevertheless from time to time occur syntheses of highly sophisticated artificial and abstract systems with an intense observation and understanding of nature, in which neither gain the upper hand but achieve a perfect balance. This is found in the Greek reliefs of the Parthenon and in simple gravestones. One naturally expects the best work of any period to be outstanding, and if we can keep our minds free from scholastic prejudices we find that there is no period of history without fine works of art being made somewhere. But it is a measure of the standard of Greek art and civilisation that simple, unsigned tombstones for the grave of an ordinary woman can be of such care and beauty.

If we read in our newspapers today of a quarrel between philosophers and artists, we should not consider it a news item of much importance. Certainly we should think of it as having no bearing on everyday life. Philosophy is a special study of ideas by a tiny minority who seem to be remote and unworldly.

Originally, however, philosophy meant the study of all ideas, and was a driving force in religion and politics and very much bound up with governments and power. Socrates' death in 399 BC bears witness to this fact. Socrates, or rather Plato, who certainly put a lot of his own ideas into the arguments of Socrates that he recorded, also said some very important things about the art of his day which are still relevant.

Socrates himself was a sculptor-mason who gave up his trade for that of critic and teacher of ideas. He lived during the war between Athens and Sparta that brought classical Greece to an end, and took a turn of duty in the Athenian army, where he seemed to be completely indifferent to hardship or danger. He lived to see certain radical changes occur in Greek art, particularly sculpture, and he violently disapproved of them.

He and his philosophers considered that they had been betrayed. The rulers of Athens paid lip service to the ideals that they taught, but in practice followed any expedient line thought to be the easiest solution. Massacres and the betrayal of alliances turned foreign opinion against Athens while she boasted of her great civilisation and rational outlook. The philosophers turned away from the chaos of everyday life to an ideal world of the mind. This world was not one of escape to contemplation, but a very active mental laboratory where all problems could be considered in their true light. Here, in mechanics, friction did not interfere with motion, and equally in moral philosophy only reason unadulterated by sentiment or emotion was important.

The sculptor, once the spokesman in stone of the philosopher, was abandoned with the rest of the everyday world. To work with one's hands was socially far below working with one's mind. Sculptors turned for patronage from the educated philosophers to the rich merchant. They produced work that appealed not to the mind but to the emotions, and a popular style, compounded of realism and sentiment, resulted.

Plato makes Socrates attack this sculpture in terms familiar to modern readers. He deemed that highly realistic and emotional sculpture seduced the minds of unthinking people, and turned their thoughts away from the ideal and abstract. It was immoral to receive emotions and sensations at second-hand without the hazards of experience. This argument is very close to that which in some quarters is used to attack sex and violence in films and television.

Plato would have allowed certain limited forms of abstract art. He approved of the form and purpose of Egyptian art, but held that the purest forms of all are certain regular geometrical solids. All forms in nature are these forms modified. Further, he says that aesthetics, or feelings, are not special but shared by man with the lowest forms of animal life. Man at the mercy of his feelings is a wild animal. Feelings and emotions must be controlled by reason and the intellect.

Thus very early on in the history of art and thought, we find the same arguments used today for and against abstract art and realism expressed in very clear terms. Needless to say the argument in favour of Plato's pure abstraction found little popular support, and sculpture became a competition in virtuosity.

Still, looking at Hellenistic sculpture we find ourselves quite sympathetic to Plato's viewpoint. It does seem to be decadent. Perhaps it is too smooth, too beautiful. The males are so elegant as to be slack in form. Their features are so regular as to be both cold and characterless, pretty rather than handsome. The females become coyly erotic. Sentiment replaces emotion.

From time to time these works have been very highly regarded and held to be the key to ideal beauty. The pose of the *Apollo Belvedere* has been quoted time and again by portrait painters to flatter their patrons, and the *pudenta* pose of the *Venus de Medici* reappears in medieval church sculpture, in Botticelli's *Venus* and in modern corset advertisements.

Hellenistic sculpture was just what seemed to be needed by the Romans, the inheritors of Greek civilisation. Certain fundamental differences in ideas between the two civilisations are highlighted in the sculpture that they produced.

At their peak the Greeks were thoughtful idealists who preferred logical argument to actual experiment. The Romans were practical and pragmatic; they would rather act than think. Precedent was

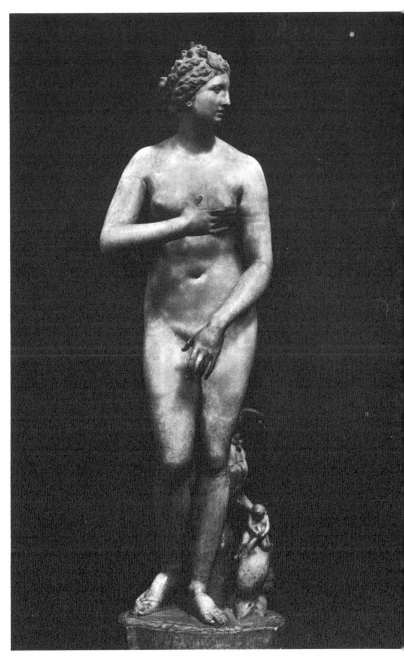

Venus de Medici, 2nd century B.C.
Uffizi, Florence *Photo : Alinari*

the foundation of Roman law and Roman society. Judgments became law, and these laws in turn would be modified by successive circumstances until changes in society forced a change in law. The foundation of Rome was a peculiar affair of a few Italian families. Rome always grew more by settlement and adoption than by generation, and adoption into a Roman family or clan was an essential honour for an immigrant. Thus one's ancestors became an affair of great importance, and reverence for them approached ancestor-worship. This cult led to a demand for portraiture, both painted and carved. The Roman portrait busts are among the finest sculptures produced at any period. A beautiful degree of balance was arrived at between an abstract language of form and the actual likeness of the person portrayed.

A sculptor did not learn to carve by copying a living model, but by learning to carve details from other sculpture. He would learn how

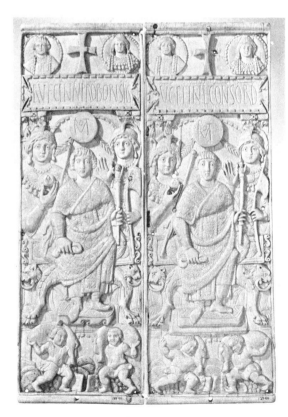

Consular Diptych of Rufus Germadius Probus Orestes, c. 530 A.D., ivory, 13.875 × 4.6 ins (each leaf)
Victoria and Albert Museum, London, *Crown copyright*

to carve the standard symbols for hair, or a nose, lips, or an eye, with its constant cross-section of ridged lids over the sphere of the ball. The pupil was represented by a finely engraved circle, in which was carved quite a deep channel in the shape of a rounded U. This left a solid circle of stone in the centre of the pupil, with a little neck of stone at the top, a clever device for simulating the transparency of the pupil and its corresponding highlight.

Once the carver had this language of form at his finger tips, he could concentrate on obtaining his likeness without thought of how he should do so. It is this established language of form that is the basis of what we all-embracingly call 'classical' sculpture. In some matters the Romans showed a lack of self-confidence, a long-standing feeling of inferiority. Fine engineers, they hastened to cover up their marvellous domed and arched structures with a veneer of inappropriate columnar decoration, as if naked structure was indecent, forgetting that the architectural decoration they used was originally purely structural. In the same way they considered that their fine portrait busts were necessary furnishings, rather than works of art.

When it came to the latter, they preferred to import debased marble copies of Greek bronzes churned out for the rich Roman market, or sentimental Hellenistic work, suitable background art against which a wealthy Roman merchant could take his ease without having to think too much.

Even a highly educated and intelligent man such as the Emperor Hadrian thought that he was improving upon Greek sculpture by having elaborate copies made in which flesh and blood, hair, draperies, eyes, lips and teeth were imitated in natural coloured and veined marbles.

Generally speaking the Romans worked in coarser and softer limestones than the Greek pentelic marbles. To speed up production they used edged chisels in oblique cross-hatched strokes, and used drills whenever possible to honeycomb surplus stone for easier cutting away. The flat chiselling can be both hard and coarse when compared to the Greek use of the punch, and the comparison is obvious in idealised abstracted portrayals of the human figure. In the realm of portraiture, where there was no precedent or comparison, the sculptors' form evolved from their technique and achieved the synthesis essential to a true work of art.

Symmachi panel, c. 400 A.D.,
ivory, 11.6 × 4.75 ins
Victoria and Albert Museum, London,
Crown copyright

The period between the end of the Roman Empire and the revival of classicism in the fifteenth century, tended to be looked upon by scholars as a sort of cultural desert. The dramatisation of the fall of Rome obscures the fact that a great many of the surviving buildings of Rome with their attendant sculptures were erected during the declining years of the Empire. Caracalla's reign as emperor was decadent and short, and yet saw the building of his enormous pleasure house, popularly called 'baths' but containing shops, library, lecture hall, theatre and every kind of entertainment. The invading, looting barbarians thought of themselves as the inheritors rather than the destroyers of Rome.

Classical learning and classical form was too fundamental, too strong simply to die overnight. To a sculptor there was still only one way to carve, however deformed his attempts might become. The major change is in scale, not style or language. What becomes impossible after the age of Constantine, the first Christian emperor (A.D. 313), is the carrying out and the maintenance of large scale works, through the breakdown of all organisation. The exception was in the new eastern capital, Constantinople, where a combination of Greek thought and Roman technology produced the great church of Santa Sophia, and sent back cultural missionaries all over Europe via the ports of Ravenna and Venice. The large scale works of art are the mosaic murals; 'paintings' one ought rather to call them, for decoration is an inadequate word to describe these pictures painstakingly built up in tiny tesserae, pieces of marble and semi-precious stone, coloured glass and glass-embedded gold and silver leaf.

Sculpture became a miniaturist's art. The carver's tools were the fine drill and knife-like chisels, his medium ivory and bone. Christian theology replaced philosophy, and his patrons were Christian princes and the Church itself. The Parthenon was turned into a Christian basilica, and the frieze and metopes, which showed angels fighting with strange half-horse demons, were popularly believed to have been inspired by the artist-apostle, St Luke.

The churches established rules for artists to work by and a rigid Byzantine formula was evolved which, in eastern Europe, persisted almost unchanged until the nineteenth century.

Its characteristics are an elongation of form, a persistent sinuous

outline, and a certain heaviness of drawing, particularly noticeable in such details as eyes and hands. The figures in the reliefs appear to float in mid air, their feet pointing downwards.

All these factors combine to give Byzantine ivory figures an unearthly quality, a heightened spirituality. This may have been in part due to the requirements of the Church, but was also due to the carvers partly taking their models from the mosaicists. In the latter medium a linear outlined quality is a necessity, and the heavily underlined, staring eyes are particularly noticeable. However, this cosmetic fashion, for so it seems to be, is observable in some pre-Christian painting in the eastern Mediterranean. The downward pointing feet are due to the artist changing his viewpoint when drawing feet, as much as to a spiritual formula. Beneath the Byzantine elaboration and heaviness, however, the Graeco-Roman model clearly shows through.

In the fourth century in Rome there was something of a revival of pure classicism, and some notable ivories date from the time of the Emperor Julian, who endeavoured to rebuild a Rome based on pre-Christian philosophy.

The ivory panel of the Symmachi is completely classical in thought and execution – in everything but scale. This revival also influenced Christian artists, and the ivory panel of the Archangel from the first half of the sixth century is also classical in form and thought. These examples of the persistence of classical form are not isolated phenomena.

By the time of Charlemagne's attempt to rebuild a Christian Roman Empire, Byzantine artists had workshops all over France and Germany, and were training native artists in them. A minor rebirth of classicism took place under Charlemagne comparable to that of the eighth century in Rome.

Ivory covers for liturgical books were produced in such quantity that a great many have survived to this day, despite their fragility. Quite distinct groups of work are identifiable, based on secular or monastic workshops. One such is the 'Ada' group, so called after the Abbess Ada who commissioned some of the group's best work. A notable example of a book cover by the Ada group has three sections. The main part of the panel has three figures standing in architectural niches. The concept is classical, so is the handling of the figures and drapery, and the design of the architectural detail. Above the figures is an antique pagan image adapted to

Copy of book cover from Ada
Group, ivory (original in Vatican)
Victoria and Albert Museum, London
Crown Copyright

Christian use: two flying angels bearing a wreath. Formerly th
would have contained the imperial eagle or emperor's bust. He
we find the head of Christ. At the bottom of the panel are scen
from the Nativity and the angel appearing to the watchir
shepherds. These in turn derive from antique narrative relie
such as those on Trajan's column. Here the language of classicis
speaks louder than that of Byzantium

Chapter 7 Romanesque and Gothic

South of the Alps there was an unspoken tradition from the end
of the Roman Empire through the Middle Ages until the Renaissance,
hardly intruded upon by northern Gothic form. Surrounded by the
ruins and fragments of Roman civilisation, the inhabitants of Italy
always thought of themselves as heirs to Rome, and used what they
saw about them long before the fifteenth century. A collection
of Roman marbles at Pisa served as guide to the Pisano family of
sculptors in the thirteenth century.

In 1260 Nicolo Pisano carved, signed and dated a pulpit in the
baptistery at Pisa. One of the relief panels contains four scenes.
The dominant scene is the Nativity ; subsidiary to it but contained
within the same frame are the Annunciation to the Virgin, and
the angel appearing to the shepherds. Tucked away and below
is the birth of the Virgin herself. The poses are monumental. The
handling of form is completely classical. The main figure of the
Virgin is a reclining Roman matron straight from an antique tomb.
The carving is hard with a clear, crisp edge. The folds are slightly
angular, the planes clearly defined. The technique used is some-
what akin to a woodcarver's. A flat edged chisel was the tool,
held at an acute angle to the surface of the stone.

33

The apparent inconsistencies of scale and incidental sequence in the panel are relevant and important. Both artist and beholder knew the chronological order of events in the Gospel, and could read the events as such without confusion. Even so, the two simultaneous figures of the Virgin occurring in incidents widely separated by time actually overlap each other in the carving. The size of the figures does not depend upon their relative positions in space, but upon a hieratic order of importance. If it appears ambiguous to us, it is because we are measuring it against another scale of space and time quite different from the medieval idea of the natural order of things. There is a lack of historical definition in the modern sense. This is also apparent in the philosophy of the day. Contemporary with Pisano, St Thomas Aquinas could write a commentary in the margin of his Plato as if arguing with a living person. Time does not enter into his argument, there is no suggestion of a philosopher of 1,000 years before being out-of-date. The ideas are alive, and to be judged in their own right. All that Plato lacked was Divine Revelation.

Pisano took other classical models, too. A Hercules, complete with lion-skin and club, in the pose of the *Farnese Hercules* becomes a symbol of fortitude; the penitent Magdalen, cloaked by her own hair, has the pose of the *Medici Venus*.

Pisano's son, Giovanni, followed his father. At about 1310 Giovanni finished a similar pulpit at Pistoia, where the panels are flanked by seated sybils. These were greatly admired by Michelangelo and formed the models for his own sybils of the Sistine ceiling.

The one thing that the Gothic sculptors of northern Europe have in common with their southern contemporaries is the same attitude towards space and time, a feeling of past, present and future being one. Their experience of Roman rule and Roman art and architecture was provincial. They were not surrounded by a classical past. Eastern influence was as strong as Roman.

It was Byzantine glass workers who settled at Limoges by the ninth century and founded the workshops from which stained glass was to come. The pointed arch was an Eastern invention. The Byzantine elongation of form and the floating figure which originated partly from technical reasons, were most suited aesthetically to the strong, vertical emphasis in Gothic building. The word emphasis is important. Gothic buildings were meant to

Opposite page
Pieta, Italian painted
woodcarving, c. 1450
Collection Blair Hughes-Stanton

The Visitation, about 1250
Rheims Cathedral *Photo : Giraudon*

look taller than they really are. In actual height they are surpassed
by many Romanesque buildings, and the whole west façade of
Notre Dame in Paris could well fit inside the Pantheon in Rome.
Consequently elongation in sculpture was considered a necessity,
rather than a matter of choice. Although this verticality and attenua-
tion of form gives a heightened sense of the spiritual in Gothic,
this effect has been much exaggerated by commentators in the
past, particularly under the influence of Romantic writers of the
nineteenth century.

Gothic sculpture is neither morbid nor emaciated. It is not the
result of emotional mysticism or pietical hysteria. Gothic form

is not agonised in an anthropomorphic manner; in fact, there is very little direct portrayal of any sort of physical suffering. This is entirely limited to scenes of the Last Judgment, and there are surprisingly few portrayals of martyrdom.

Gothic sculpture has a detached serenity comparable to that of the archaic Greek. There are strong parallels. Both Greek and medieval thinkers were in their own way idealists, who would rather pursue an intellectual argument to a logical end than carry out physical experiments. To both the real world was not this earthly compromise. The teachings of Aristotle were approved by the Church and became part of scholastic dogma.

Gothic sculpture has a remarkably wide range, from the expression of a clear but otherworldly spirituality to an extreme naturalism based on the direct observation of nature.

At Chartres the porches of the twelfth and thirteenth centuries are adorned by column-like figures clad in draperies which are almost fluting. The carver's technique in punching out the form was very similar to the Greek sculptor's. However, instead of using a rubbing stone to finish off, a range of metal rasps and flat chisels were used. At Rheims the mid-thirteenth-century carvings are more fluid. The remarkable sculptured figures of the Visitation might have been taken from classical models. Where the sculptor could have found antique statues to study, and what they could have been, it is impossible to say. They are just as likely to have been the sculptor's own original idea, produced not by a knowledge of the past but by parallel conditions to the past.

France was the generating centre of northern European sculpture. The remarkable portrait figures at Naumburg were certainly carved in the workshops there by sculptors who were French taught, and particularly at Rheims. There are twelve figures in the choir at Naumburg, supposed portraits of the founders of the cathedral. Although they are mythical likenesses, the sculptor worked from living models, clothing his figures in his own contemporary costume of the mid-to-late thirteenth century. The heads are full of character, absolute likenesses yet expressing only serene repose. The head of Uta in particular has a beauty that strikes one as being of one's own time.

This realism is not so unexpected when one analyses the foliate decoration of much religious building. Here minute plants are enlarged into roof bosses a yard across without destroying or distorting their natural form. The controlling factor is that of geometry. The accidents of nature are ignored, the irregularities straightened out. The structure of the plant forms are analysed and the carvings built on that foundation.

In mentioning the foliated decoration of column capitals, one is made aware of their descent from the Corinthian column of antiquity. The thread is strong. In spite of technical innovation the Gothic cathedral plan is still essentially the Roman basilica, the Gothic west front is the Roman triumphal arch regenerated.

The division of the history of art into labelled periods such as 'Middle Ages' and 'Renaissance' is convenient for chapter headings, but the people concerned at these times were not always aware of sudden changes, and however dramatic these changes seem to be to the retrospective observer, they did not happen overnight. Nevertheless, there is a definite watershed between the end of the fourteenth and beginning of the fifteenth centuries. The change was labelled the 'Renaissance' or rebirth, partly as a derogatory reflection on the Middle Ages at a time when Gothic was a synonym for barbaric.

The rebirth was that of classical learning, art and architecture. Artists and scholars were held to have suddenly turned once more to forgotten or neglected classical examples, and to have coupled this rediscovery with a new, detached scientific study of the natural world. This is true, but it is also true of the Middle Ages. Classical examples were never entirely forgotten. In the purest Gothic art they were transformed; in Romanesque Italy they were often directly copied. Artists worked directly from nature too, with a clear and objective vision. Nor can they be accused of technical incompetence; the technology of the Middle Ages was second to none. In philosophy the use of scientific logic was never abandoned, but often abused.

There are big differences, however, and very important ones, for our present-day ideas are still based on these changes. The Pisano panel of the Nativity gives a clue to some of these changes. In the panel we find all the technical accomplishments at one time held to be the prerogative of the Renaissance. The fluent competence, the intelligent use of classical models are there, but by post-Renaissance standards the panel is confused. It contradicts one popular view of medieval church art: that such works were a popular picture story of the Bible for the illiterate. The contents of this panel, and many other similar works, can only be interpreted as a logical sequence of events by someone who is already familiar with the story being told. A person who had no previous knowledge of the Gospel story might be forgiven for thinking that these were simultaneous events in the same place, involving several different groups of people. We can only assume that neither the sculptor nor his patrons were concerned with this difficulty at all. So it follows that their attitude towards space and time was very different from that of ours today. We expect to see in a picture or carving one space and one time related to our own. One thing happens to one person at a time, and a person or thing cannot be in two places at once.

The medieval artists and thinkers also knew that events happen in sequence and that people in everyday life cannot be in two places at once, but they never concerned themselves with the definition of space and time in such a way. Indeed, such a definition of space and time is related to the idea of here and now. In an age when philosophy was concentrated on the eternal and ideal, such a definition would have been thought to be irrelevant.

We might therefore say that the Renaissance marks the beginning of a new demand for definition in all fields. This grew out of philosophy. The philosopher's tools are words, his method is argument. In particular his universal language was Latin. Before argument could begin, agreement had to be reached on the meaning of words, and the structure of statements clarified. To do this philosophers had constantly to turn away from the Church's approved reading to other Roman models. This combined search for meaning and a new investigation of classical writing grew and spread to other fields, to the natural sciences and to art. Upon it is based the philosophy we call humanism, and the movement called the Renaissance.

Ambiguity in language became undesirable; so did ambiguity in art. The formulation of the rules of geometrical perspective was part of the process. Their use in painting meant one space and one time in each picture, related to the spectator in an intimate personal way. However remote the events portrayed, they took place in an organised system that the onlooker could meet with a feeling of recognition.

There is no parallel in the development of sculpture as obvious as the introduction of perspective. But the new self-awareness of which perspective was a part, is even more striking in the development of sculpture.

The Swiss philosopher-historian Jacob Burckhardt wrote that the Renaissance signified the emergence of the individual out of anonymity. Today we take a different view of medieval anonymity. In fact a far greater number of names of artists and architects is recorded than Burckhardt knew. Nevertheless, it is not just a matter of unsigned works that makes for anonymity. Generally speaking we can say that much Egyptian, Graeco-Roman, or medieval sculpture is more similar than different. In each period there was a great deal of work that is of a consistent, good, average standard, based upon commonly observed rules of sculpture.

This anonymity ended with the Renaissance. The sculptor asserted himself as an individual. A strong rivalry developed, not only among artists but among their wealthy patrons, whose understanding of art was at least equalled by their pride of possession. Man was unique, and every ambitious man had to prove his own unique quality. Artists rivalled each other in innovation and virtuosity, and the popular accounts of their lives are full of violent rivalries and campaigns against one another. It was this competitive world that produced Michelangelo (1475–1564), whose work and life epitomises the Renaissance artist. He was a tough, touchy, quarrelsome man, jealous of his dignity and status. He learned his stone cutting among masons, then served his apprenticeship in a painter's studio, getting an all-round training. Very early on he was noticed by Lorenzo de Medici, who gave him studio space of his own and took him into the household, where his education was furthered among humanist scholars who also enjoyed Medicean patronage. Michelangelo was to spend most of his life in either Rome or Florence, alternating between the two as the political power of his patrons fluctuated. Already impatient by nature, Michelangelo's temper was not improved by the constant interruptions to his work and life occasioned by being at the mercy of political events.

He was an aggressive artist. His drawing and painting, modelling and sculpture all show attack upon the medium. When his figures are at rest, their form is not. A contemplative figure will have a strong twist or exaggerated *contrapposto* in the torso.

There is a marked similarity in appearance between the violent cross-hatching in Michelangelo's drawing and the criss-crossed chisel marks on the unfinished portions of his sculpture. Using pointed and clawed chisels he tended to work obliquely to the form, holding his chisel almost tangentially. The strokes cross each other at all angles round a protrusion or boss. The chisel marks run extremely deep in the rougher passages. The sculptor must have removed considerable pieces of marble at each blow

MICHELANGELO : Pietà, c. 1500
St. Peter's, Rome *Photo : Alinari*

MICHELANGELO : Slave,
originally intended for the tomb
of Julius II c. 1513–16
Louvre, Paris *Photo : Giraudon*

in the initial stages. To do this requires great physical force, an presupposes supreme knowledge of stone and confidence of form on the part of the sculptor. Limbs were left webbed together for strength and support until a late stage. Unlike the Greek sculptors Michelangelo finished his carvings piecemeal, sometimes taking a detail almost to final finish long before the roughing out was completed. The final finish was achieved with a rasp, pumice powder, various grades of sand, and rubbing stone. The early work, such as the *Pieta* in St Peter's of 1498, has a highly polished surface. Later, as Michelangelo grew more confident, he not only preferred a more matt finish, but deliberately left quite conspicuous work-marks.

He used clay and wax for sketches, but never cast in metal Surviving models show the same forceful attack on both medium and form. His knowledge of anatomy was considerable, but is more easily seen in the drawings than the sculpture. In the drawings the tonal shading is built up by a series of successively correcting layers, not by copying the shadows on the form of the model. It is this drawing from the inside out, so to speak, that relates directly to the sculptor's bold attack. It also affected his manner of carving to a certain extent. He seems to have carved his way into a block as if following the natural form that he was creating. For example in a limb he tended to carve along a muscle rather than round it as if following the striated layers that he knew to be there in a living body. The abdominal muscles are cut with interleaving strokes, again as in living form.

It has been argued that an over-awareness of anatomy led him to masculine mannerism in his carving of the female figures on the Medicean tombs in Florence. This seems unlikely. Michelangelo was much too self-conscious an artist to allow any special study to lead him into errors of judgment. If his symbolic female figures look masculine, then we may be certain that he meant them to be so. Whether this had symbolic content or was a private, wilful gesture must be deduced from a more detailed study of the sculptor, and in particular of the imagery used in his notes and poetry.

DONATELLO : Equestrian statue Erasmo da Narni, called Gattamelata, 1443–53 Padua *Photo : Alinari*

Chapter 9 Baroque

While allowing Michelangelo the archetypical place among Renaissance sculptors, mention must be made of a consistent sculptural development through the fifteenth and sixteenth centuries, in particular in casting in bronze. This increase of skill in casting techniques stems from the demands made on cannon founders for the late medieval and early Renaissance wars. Artillery manufacture demanded the careful control of alloys used, the handling of sufficient quantities of molten metal for large one-piece castings and hollow castings of great accuracy with no flaws, pockets or blow-holes in them.

While the carver patiently and carefully removed masses of surplus stone chip by chip, the sculptor in bronze could freely add to or decrease his volumes, twist and turn his axes, and, knowing that his bronze had greater resistance to shear and fracture than crystalline stone, let his statues balance on a single point support. All this led to a gradual refinement both of volumes and gestures. Grace became a sculptural cult. In the early transitional phases

ANDREA DEL VERROCHIO:
Monument to Condottiere
Colleoni, 1479–88
Venice *Photo: Anderson*

Donatello (1386–1466) combined Gothic severity with a tau
lithe elasticity of form. The popularity of the boy David is typic
of the early Renaissance emphasis on youth and intelligenc
Donatello's bronze *David* (c. 1435) is a true Renaissance wor
Elegant *contrapposto* has replaced the Gothic four-square quali
of his earlier work. The Venetians commissioned Donatello to scu
a bronze monument to their *condottiere* Gattamelata. This work,
1446–7, was the first major equestrian monument to be carrie
out since the Roman statue of Marcus Aurelius, which wa
Donatello's prototype. This was also the first great secular publ
monument of the Renaissance and set a pattern for the futur
At the end of the century Verrocchio succeeded Donatello wi
another David figure and with the monument to another Venetia
condottiere, Colleoni, using both the *Gattamelata* and the *Marc*
Aurelius as his models. Verrocchio's famous pupil, Leonardo c
Vinci, would have overtopped both with his giant equestria
bronze of Francesco Sforza of Milan, the largest bronze castin
ever attempted to that date. The model was finished, but aft

endless debate on the finances of casting, it was destroyed during the French occupation of Milan, being shot to pieces by archers at target practice.

The new demand for public secular sculpture, to the glory of a hero or for corporate and civic pride, was paralleled by a demand for small scale sculpture for the houses of wealthy patrons. Goldsmiths and metalworkers turned out miniature sculptures for lamps, inkstands, door furniture and small fountains, all of a very high standard and mostly made by the lost wax process. Chief among these artist craftsmen was Benvenuto Cellini (1500–71). His major works show a transition as important as that at the beginning of the Renaissance but not, unfortunately, as fruitful. His *Perseus* of 1545–54 is the successor to Donatello's *David*, and is based purely on classical mythology with no lip service being paid to the Church. It is a work of great technical virtuosity, with a tendency to florid decoration that would not be out of place in a nineteenth-century French salon. It is not quite decadent, but foreshadows the decadence which followed almost immediately.

DONATELLO: David with the
head of Goliath, c. 1435
Museo Nazionale, Florence
Photo: Alinari

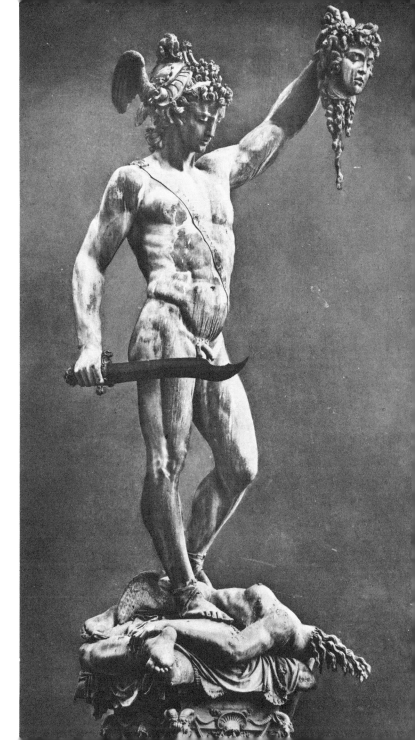

BENVENUTO CELLINI:
Perseus, c. 1554
Loggia dei Lauzi Florence, *Photo : Alinari*

Self-awareness inevitably leads to disillusion. A giant will, such as that of Michelangelo, can survive the despair to which his own search for truth may bring him, but lesser men have to find a refuge. Michelangelo's successors inherited his shattering influence without his strength. They therefore tried to temper confusion with theory, evolving formulae for ideal beauty to satisfy their own Renaissance rationalism. This self-conscious search for laws of aesthetics led to a preoccupation with technique and a desire for purity and flawlessness in form. Finish became a measure of proficiency. Carvers were strongly influenced by bronze casting and emulated the flexibility of the latter. Grace became equated with softness and fluidity, and elegance with exaggerated elongation. Beauty could only exist where there was pleasantness, and was a prerogative of luxury. Beauty was also strongly associated with the sexual and erotic.

Even in his religious work Lorenzo Bernini (1598–1690) could not clearly distinguish between *eros* and *agape*. His *The Ecstasy of St Theresa* (1646) is full of the pagan symbolism of Cupid and a virginal victim. He also mistook the nature of emotion for that of mere sentiment. His technique was that of a virtuoso, and clearly derived from bronze rather than stone models.

These are the symptoms of a decline in sculpture from that of the heroic phase of the Renaissance. Looked at in detail there is strong evidence of formal decadence in the sculpture of the high and late Renaissance, the periods of Baroque and Rococo. However, if individual works lack intensity of both form and idea, these deficiencies are not so important in an age which was primarily that of public sculpture, in churches, palaces, cities and great gardens. An enormous amount of sculpture was mass-produced with an aim of total effect. The work was not intended for scrutiny or for the mind to dwell upon at length. Fountains were focal points at an intersection of busy streets, the rows of white statuary were to be seen against dark cypress or yew, or, as at Versailles, against fully grown planes and chestnuts as squarely clipped as a box-hedge border. Formal defects and symbolic absurdities are unimportant in these monumental fountains, or in the groups of figures adorning the parapet and piers of a fine bridge. In a Baroque church the theatrical framing of the High Altar called for a certain coarseness of technique which went well with the dramatic gestures of the floating figures, the blowing draperies and violent poses.

Seated saint with cross: from the
Mercy altar, begun 1743,
completed 1771
Pilgrim's Church, Vierzehnheiligen
Photo: Marburg

Technical virtuosity pursued for its own sake does not spoil the
thrill of recognition that we can experience when we look at the
highly naturalistic portraiture of the period, when the sculptor so
liked to show off his ability to carve stone into a lace collar.

The final collapse came with the Industrial Revolution of the mid-
eighteenth to late nineteenth centuries. Classical education had
exercised a certain restraint and gave late Renaissance sculpture
much of its purpose. However, a classical education could no longer
cope with the necessity of teaching the new sciences, and became
an academic exercise. Mechanisation and mass-production brought
its own problems. Previously the size, elaboration and time-con-
suming technical difficulties had partly governed the cost of a

LORENZO BERNINI:
St Theresa in ecstasy,
1645–52
Cornaro Chapel,
Santa Maria della Vittoria, Rome
Photo: Alinari

work of art. Through a simple material misapprehension, complication became firmly equated with expense and luxury in the nineteenth-century mind.

In a like manner realism was equated with an exact reproduction of the material appearance of things. Lack of education in form led the public to demand that a work of art be immediately recognisable. This, coupled with the failure of classical education, led to sculptural absurdities. On one hand these may be of the order of Canova's giant nude statue of Napoleon as an early nineteenth-century Achilles, or of Pauline Bonaparte as a reclining Venus; on the other hand to the clothing of respectable nineteenth-century statesmen in Roman senatorial togas, or else casting them in bronze complete with silk hat, umbrella and boots.

The purity of smooth white marble seems to have had a literal association with purity of mind to the Victorian eye. An age which has almost become synonymous with prudery filled private conservatories and public halls with sugary female nudes, whose coy timidity coupled with realism untempered by the classical language of form, seem to achieve that very indecency that the nineteenth century sought to avoid.

Such works were mass-produced. Carvers rarely worked straight off into the stone. Generally the piece of sculpture was modelled to full size or preferably larger, and as it was built up measuring points were built into the clay or plaster. By means of proportionate dividers these points were used as datum marks to produce an exact copy of the model in stone. Thus stone carving became completely dominated by modelling technique, and absolute smoothness of surface and accuracy of finish was held to be evidence of a job well done.

Attempts were made to build copying machines to work on the pointing principle in order to mass-produce sculpture. The engineer James Watt, famous for his improvement of the steam engine, spent the better part of his life trying to perfect a 'following' machine for producing sculpture. Such machines using Watt's principles do in fact exist today, but the sculptured forms they produce are enormous steel dies for stamping out car bodies.

This preoccupation with the surface of sculpture was the bane of the nineteenth century. It may be seen most clearly by comparing the drawings of Michelangelo with those of Alfred Stevens (1817–75). Stevens was a skilled draughtsman and sculptor who took Michelangelo as his ideal. If we look at a typical Michelangelo drawing we see that the tone or shading which gives the drawing its three-dimensional quality, is the result of a process of continuous correction. The drawing is made up of a series of successive layers, working from the inside of the form to the outside, each following layer becoming darker.

Stevens' drawings are entirely of the surface. His modelling is simply of the actual shadow crossing the contour. There is little or no visible correction, a cold perfection of form being aimed at 'first time', as if this were a moral obligation on the part of the artist. Consequently whereas Michelangelo could bring a pen and ink drawing or a carved piece of marble to life, Stevens and his fellows have the opposite effect, that of reducing living form to dead.

There are many simple and material reasons for the fact that it wa the painter who took the initiative in developing the visual arts i the latter half of the nineteenth century. The painter's materials ar portable and more tractable, he does not need so much room, hi materials are cheaper and his output faster than that of the sculpto The painter does not have so much capital tied up in any singl piece of work. He can sell at rock-bottom prices to patrons wh are ready to take risks, and does not depend so much on commis sions. If the patron at a later stage considers that he has made mistake, it is easier for him to store or sell a canvas than a heav piece of bronze or stone. It is also easier for the painter to com promise, and many a painter has steered a fluctuating cours between being level with public taste to being well ahead of without anyone doubting his integrity.

The mid-nineteenth century sculptor could not take such risks. H could not afford to have a studio filled with unsold work in th way that a painter like Cézanne could. Thus it is only towards th end of the century and after the Impressionist painters had becom well established, that we find a comparable change taking plac in sculpture. Indeed, the change was partly due to the sculptura work produced by painters such as Degas and Renoir.

Their work, however, and the reforming movement in sculptur generally, was not a direct translation of Impressionist ideas int sculptural form, as may be said of some post-Impressionist work The sculpture of Degas and Renoir is allied much more to thei drawing than painting, springing parallel to their painting rathe than arising out of it. To them their sculptures, modelled and no carved, were three-dimensional drawings in space.

The giant of the sculptural Renaissance of the late nineteenth an early twentieth centuries is Rodin (1840–1917). He was a tru primitive, not in the sense that some naïve artists are labelle primitives, but in the Socratic sense. (Socrates was the untaugh philosopher who shattered the Academics by his system of direc question and answer, and who owes his reputation as a forma philosopher to his biographer and interpreter, the scholastic Plato. Cézanne was another such primitive who, without knowing i founded a rationalist school of painting. Rodin turned straight bacl to Michelangelo, asking questions of the Master's work as

EDGAR DEGAS: The Little Dancer, aged 14, 1880–81, bronze with muslin
skirt and satin hair-ribbon, height excluding base 39 ins
Tate Gallery, London *By courtesy of the Trustees*

AUGUSTE RODIN: L'Age
d'Airain (The Age of Bronze),
1875–77, bronze, height
71.25 ins
Tate Gallery, London *By courtesy of the
Trustees*

Michelangelo himself were present to advise his latter-day disciple. Rodin's search ranged from dramatic realism – the sculptor was accused of making the male figure *Bronze Age* from a plaster cast of a live model – to an aggressively deliberate roughness of form that almost overcomes the content of his sculpture.

Rodin took Michelangelo's exposed technique and unfinished surfaces as signs of sculptural honesty. In Rodin's hands these were pursued for their own sake, becoming ends in themselves. The public, brought up on the principle of value for money and regarding finish as a measure of value, were properly outraged, and Rodin's work, with the tool marks and thumb prints left in the clay, was associated with the loose techniques of the Impressionist painters. This looseness of technique is not really similar, for that of Rodin springs from very different sources.

Every period of painting has its practitioners of bravura handling but this is not so in sculpture. Rodin's handling springs from a personal moral conviction, that of achieving true integrity by swiftly translating into wax and clay the inner and forceful convictions of the moment. He described his methods as if they were the result of a tempestuous love affair between himself and his sculpture.

Rodin's carving is not so successful. His attempt to get a sense of urgency into a technique that is slow and laborious, led him to exaggerate the differences in texture between his finished and unfinished surfaces. The effect is generally rhetorical and uncertain. The finished form becomes too shallow, reminding one of the more decadent and sentimental characteristics of Art Nouveau. Rodin's example of assault on his medium led to developments in sculpture that he would have been surprised to see. These are dealt with elsewhere. The immediate successor to Rodin was Jacob Epstein(1880–1959). He, after a long search in early life through many formal experiments with form, achieved a synthesis between the exposure of technique and a highly personal language of form with the most penetrating insight into character. The result was a series of portraits almost impossible to describe in verbal terms. Craters, ridges, seams and fissures of molten bronze combine into the most realistic portraits that have been rarely equalled in any period. Just how this vigorously worked-over mass of material becomes a head, is as difficult to define as it is to state the precise stage at which the brushwork of a bravura painter changes from

AUGUSTE RENOIR: Venus Victrix, 1914, bronze, height 72 ins
Tate Gallery, London *By courtesy of the Trustees*

AUGUSTE RODIN:
Le Baiser, 1901–04,
Pentelican marble,
71.75 × 48 × 60.25 ins
Tate Gallery, London
By courtesy of the Trustees

marks on a canvas into an illusion of solid form.

Epstein's carved work is again less successful than his modelled
His attempt to force urgency and dynamic strength into the stone
resulted in overstraining for effect, and he failed to achieve that
extraordinary synthesis between his intentions and his material
that he achieved in bronze. Latterly he fused the monumentality he
sought in carving with his mastery of modelling. These later works

seem to go back beyond the Renaissance tradition to Donatello, but on an enormous scale. The drawing never faulters. There is no superfluous gesture. The *Madonna and Child* in London, or the Coventry *St Michael and the Devil* are taut and spare.

There is a second line of realism stemming from the late nineteenth century, owing more to Degas and Renoir than to Rodin. Maillol (1861–1944), twenty years younger than Renoir and wholly a

ARISTIDE MAILLOL: Venus
with a Necklace, 1918–28,
bronze, height 69.5 ins
Tate Gallery, London *By courtesy of the
Trustees*

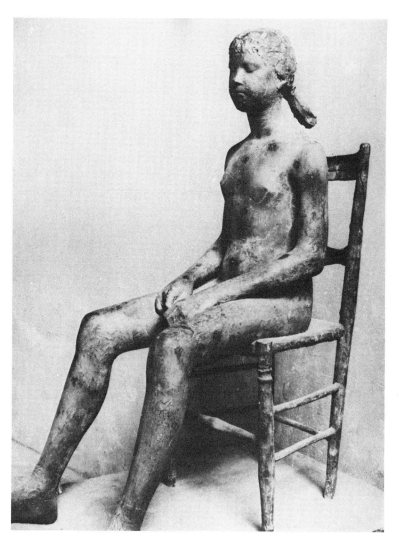

GIACOMO MANZU: Young girl
in chair, 1953–54, bronze,
height 43.5 ins
Hanover Gallery, London

sculptor, was producing monumental torsos parallel with those of
Renoir. The work of Degas (1834–1917) is leaner, more concerned
with line than volume. His bronze dancing girls are the ances-
tresses of those of Giacomo Manzu (b.1908) and Emilio Greco
(b.1915).

Both these Italian sculptors in their form and patina look back to
two different aspects of classical sculpture of the ancient world:
Manzu to the sweet severity of Greece, Greco to the voluptuous-
ness of the Graeco-Roman period.

Chapter 11 Cubism

If the link between Impressionist paintings and their contemporar
sculpture is rather intangible, and mainly limited to a certain pre
occupation with the moving figure and freedom of handling o
their respective media, the connection between Cubism in paintin
and sculpture is, on the other hand, more obvious. This is really t
be expected. In the first place Cézanne tended to relate his forms i
painting to simple solids, to the cube, sphere, cylinder and flat plane
The Cubists seized on this element in Cézanne's work and carrie
it a stage further. Early cubist portraits, landscapes and still-live
tend to look as if they were built up out of pieces of clipped ti
sheet mounted on a flat surface. The apparent depth in a cubis
picture is often not more than a few inches behind the pictur
surface, giving very much the appearance of a bas-relief.

The first true cubist pictures began to appear in about 1904. B
1909, Picasso (b. 1881) had produced his first sculpture in th
round, the bronze *Head of a Woman*. This is a direct translatio
into bronze of the artist's painted form of the period.

Now, however sculptural cubist painting may be, there is somethin
paradoxical and ambiguous about cubism in actual sculpture. T
begin with, one of the ideas at the root of cubism in painting wa
the attempt to present different aspects of the same form simul
taneously. We may say that this need not arise in sculpture, wher
we are free to move round the work and view all its aspects i
rapid succession. This ambiguity is of the same order as that i
Egyptian relief sculpture with its combination of side and fror
views together. There is something very Egyptian about Picasso'
work of this period, as was innocently pointed out by the naïv
painter Rousseau. This comes from several sources including th
ambiguity noted above, and also stems back through a long an
thropological line. Whether Picasso was directly inspired b
African sculpture, or whether common elements in African sculp
ture aroused Picasso's interest and arose out of the formal experi
ments on which he had already embarked, is not clear, even fror
the artist's own statements.

In the highly sophisticated bronze heads from west Africa, whic
are something of an artistic riddle, the Egyptian element is ver
strong. It is no less so, but not quite so obvious, in the nineteenth
century African wood carvings which Picasso admired. This cor

PABLO PICASSO: Head of
woman, 1909, bronze
S.P.A.D.E.M., Paris, 1965

Replica of a mask from the
Fang tribe of Gaboon.
The original mask was owned
by André Derain, and seen
by Picasso and Matisse. Bronze
Photo: William Fagg

respondance between African and cubist sculpture must not be taken too literally. Hostile contemporary critics thought that cubist sculpture represented a deliberate return to primitivism, an aggressive rejection of the sum total of western ideas in all realms of culture for a return to nature. In fact this did happen in sculpture, but the result was a very different kind of form from the precise planes of cubism.

Cubism, in fact, was not emotional and elemental but highly sophisticated. The forms were thought out and carefully put together. The sculptor analysed his subject, took it to pieces and rebuilt it in a form which stands outside the normal experience of space and time. It is, therefore, congruous with those previous phases of sculpture which were also concerned with eternal values, with Egyptian sculpture, much Greek, and with the Pisano pulpit panel described earlier, where events overlap and persons are duplicated.

Cubism was coincidental with changing ideas of space and time in the physical world. The physicists and mathematicians successfully demonstrated that standards of space and time are peculiar to the condition of the individual observer who makes them, and are not an absolute system existing outside local conditions. One cannot use a stronger word than coincidence to denote this relationship between art and science at the turn of the century, but the coincidence is at least as important as that of the new significance of African art.

Having pointed the way, Picasso produced very little cubist sculpture. A restless searcher after new forms in painting and sculpture, once satisfied with a new discovery he has usually left it to others to develop and consolidate.

As a language of form Cubism has persisted to one degree or another and is one of the main threads running through all modern art. The broad, simplified planes of Cubism have a monumental quality even on a small scale. Consequently, large scale monumental sculpture has made full use of this formal concept. Ossip Zadkine (b. 1890) and Jacques Lipchitz (b. 1891) have been consistent workers in this form. Henry Moore's carved screen for the roof of the Time-Life building is a recent example of the persistence of Cubism in a variant form.

The relationship between painting and sculpture has changed during the present century. In the past artists who were primarily

JACQUES LIPCHITZ:
Bather, 1923–25
Marlborough Fine Art Ltd, London

OSSIP ZADKINE: Standing Woman, 1935, stone
Stedelijk Museum, Amsterdam *Photo: Marc Vaux*

painters often turned to sculpture, and vice versa. Michelangelo achieved a complete synthesis between his sculptured figures and the painted prophets and sybils of the Sistine chapel ceiling. In the past, however, and even in the case of a painter-sculptor like Picasso, the distinction between two and three-dimensional work has always remained clear.

Today this is no longer so, and in the work of Jean Arp (b. 1887) the borderline is very fine. At one moment he is painting pictures which consist of simple cloud shapes superimposed upon one another, distinguished by line and colour. The next, he takes his superimposed forms, cuts them out of wood a few centimetres thick and literally superimposes them one on top of another, and the

VICTOR PASMORE: Relief construction in white, black and Indian red 1962, 24 × 25 ins,
Marlborough Fine Art Ltd., London

FERNAND LEGER: Children's Garden, 1960
Musée Fernand Léger Biot, © S.P.A.D.E.M., Paris, 1965
Photo: Jacques Mer, Antibes

painted ground becomes a 'base'. They are now distinguished by their own outline, by colour and by the shadows that they cast, varying in depth according to the light. Are they now relief paintings or painted reliefs?

The work of Ben Nicholson (b. 1894) is even more finely in the balance between painting and relief. Victor Pasmore (b. 1908) gradually changed from naturalistic painting – always with a strong element of geometrical design – to purely abstract three-dimensional reliefs which are also coloured. These are strongly influenced by the De Stijl movement. Pasmore relies upon ready-made textures and forms, using plastic sheetings, wooden mouldings and extruded metal sections. Latterly at Peterlee and Durham, Pasmore was involved in an experiment in town planning, both in looking at the town as a relief on a baseboard, and also in using the builder's standard materials to provide environmental sculpture at salient points.

Fernand Léger (1881–1955) realised his large, cubist figure compositions on an heroic scale in coloured ceramic reliefs, eventually intending to make enamelled bronzes. These are not on the borderline between tile and sculpture, but definitely sculpture of a most successful kind. The medium is not popular among sculptors, being most difficult to fire successfully on such a large scale. In his *Children's Garden* 1960, which was posthumously fired from a scale model left at the artist's death, the ceramic forms are as much as twenty-five feet high.

The most profound comment on painted sculpture was made by Henri Laurens (1885–1954). He was speaking of his own work, but the statement applies to all coloured sculpture to a greater or lesser degree; lesser in the case of attempted 'natural' colouring, greater in the case of synthetic, non-realistic colouring. Laurens was a great friend of Braque, and attempted to realise Cubism in sculpture. He combined paper collage, coloured wood and metal, and metal and coloured carvings. He noted that artificial colouring when strong enough cancelled out the effect of the variations of light on sculpture. 'My own aim', he stated, 'in colouring a statue is to give it its own light.'

HENRI LAURENS: Reclining Woman, 1927, stone, length 17.25 ins
Galerie Louise Leires, Paris. © A.D.A.G.P., Paris, 1965

Closely allied to Cubism in its formal language, but essentially differing in idea, was the Futurist movement. This was based on an extravagant enthusiasm for the new freedom that technology was to bring. The Futurists believed essentially in progress although their verbal enthusiasm for the amount of destruction that would have to take place before this progress was achieved sometimes overshadows the constructive foundation of the movement. The Futurists were looked upon as revolutionaries, and were proud to be thought of as such. Their outlook was very like that of the French *philosophes* of the immediate pre-revolutionary state. The *philosophes* idealised man in his natural state, the *belle sauvage*. The Futurists' *belle sauvage* was the machine with its attendant technician. They worshipped the thrill of speed and mechanical power. They saw a new aesthetic standard being set by the high degree of finish in the machines themselves, the hard polished surfaces, the precision of fitted parts, the sharply edged forms. The movement was Italian in origin. Its founders foresaw a new technological Renaissance in which Italy would again lead the world. The manifesto, published in 1909 by Marinetti, poet and philosopher of the movement, was strongly political and glorified all means of destruction as cleansing, giving man a chance to build a new world again.

Fortunately, the artists attached to the movement were more concerned with building than destroying, and made a permanent contribution to sculpture and painting. Paradoxically the attempt to put much of the philosophy into practice by the Fascists only produced an empty, rhetorical and banal neo-classical sculpture of the sort that the Futurists despised.

The Impressionists had already painted movement as a blur, people in the streets, the fluttering of flags, the wheels of vehicles. Both Cubists and Futurists were concerned with the geometrical expression of movement. A point tracing out a spiral path round a fixed centre describes something like a screw if the movement is continuous. If the movement is observed at intervals, the path appears to be stepped like a spiral staircase.

Thus the smooth transitional planes that are a feature of much modern art of the early years of the century are derived as much from conjectural paths in space as from the banal example of An

Nouveau. Equally from the same source are the sharp edged stepped planes of Cubism, together with the superimposition of different views of the same object.

Futurist painters such as Giacomo Balla (b. 1874) combined a blurred image or succession of moving images with the stepped, hard edged cubist form.

Umberto Boccioni (1882–1916) attempted to show movement through sculpture by treating the path that a moving object traces out in space as a solid. He himself described these forms as dynamic. As such they have their historical counterpart in Baroque sculpture. Both have an appeal by virtue of a paradox, that contained in the application of the adjective dynamic to an immobile piece of bronze or stone. The Baroque sculptors sought their effects by an actual realistic illusion, as in the theatre, carving flying figures and floating clouds, and making use of the play of light from concealed sources upon these forms. From Boccioni onwards, however, we find such adjectives as static and dynamic very aptly fitting completely non-representational sculpture.

The Futurist movement was shortlived. It was brought to an end by the reality of the first World War, and by post-war Italian Fascism. In any case one feels that its self-generating violence of expression, on which there was little to feed beyond the idea of continual change, was expending itself more quickly than it could regenerate.

More stable and lasting, but based on parallel sources, was Constructivism, the third great movement to spring from that fertile decade 1900–1910. The Constructivists preached change and revolution too, but by the harnessing of the world's full technological potential. They saw the future as an age of peace and plenty based on high production by labour-saving machine power, on the freedom that fast easy travel can give, and on a clean, scientifically organised world of correspondingly clean forms. The movement was closely allied to the modern movement in architecture. There was a high content of social reform in its philosophy, not one of political legislation but based on the conviction that in cleaning up the environment and giving people ideal living conditions, the corresponding reform in the social and moral codes would automatically follow.

The Constructivists took a romantic view of science and engineering. The hard cleanness of machine-produced form had the same

NAUM GABO:
Linear Construction, 1942–43,
plastic with plastic threads,
13.75 × 13.75 ins
Tate Gallery, London
By courtesy of the Trustees

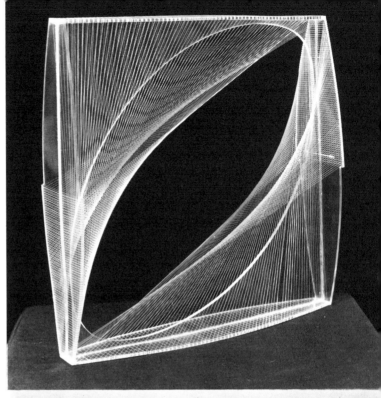

UMBERTO BOCCIONI:
Development of a bottle in
space, 1912
Museum of Modern Art, New York,
Aristide Maillol Fund

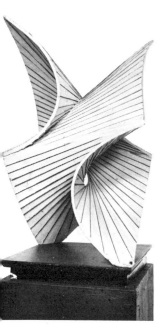

ANTOINE PEVSNER:
Developable Surface, 1938,
Peggy Guggenheim collection, Venice
by courtesy of the Arts Council
of Great Britain
Photo: R. B. Fleming & Co. Ltd

significance to them as to the Futurists. Unlike the Futurists, they based their strength of purpose upon reason and patience. To a large extent, then, Constructivism is Platonic in character. Both Cubism and Futurism were based upon a view of the actual world and were mainly figurative in nature. The Constructivists broke completely with the figurative idea, and produced purely Platonic work of ideal forms. They allied themselves at first with the Russian revolution, seeing it unconsciously as the rationalist Platonic republic where nothing would be undertaken or exist without rational cause. But the revolution was a highly emotional affair of violent loves and hates. The people did not want rational buildings but traditional palaces of their own, and they preferred heroic sculpture dedicated to themselves to ideal abstractions. The Constructivists were victims of their own enthusiasm, and disillusioned and persecuted they were forced to emigrate.

Outside Russia their ideas and sculpture met with understanding, particularly among the pioneer architects.

The work of Malevich (1878–1935) actually looks like miniature architecture. Through the school of design at Dessau, the Bauhaus, they were to have a revolutionary effect on the teaching of form.

The later work of Naum Gabo (b. 1890) and Antoine Pevsner (1886–1962) has the appearance of scientific instruments or mathematical models. Each were particularly fascinated by the development of paraboloidal surfaces, generated by a succession of straight lines moving in space across a warped plane. Gabo used strings and perspex in his demonstrations, and Pevsner clearly showed his surface developments by using welded rods.

Both use the materials of precision – stainless steel and chromium plate, talc, perspex and glass – in rods, sheets and cones. The work is carefully constructed to very fine limits. Any evidence of handwork is eliminated. There is an immediate correspondence to those mathematical solids made in the late nineteenth century to demonstrate theorems in three-dimensional co-ordinate geometry. These sculptures, however, are not mathematical models. The sculptor takes the language of the mathematician and uses it to create a poem, not a theorem, as the poet may take scientific terms and use them to describe images of his own. The work of Gabo and Pevsner is dynamic. The curved planes represent the successive positions of lines moving through space, in the same

MAX BILL: Endless Loop I, 1947–49, gilded copper on crystalline base,
height 9.75 × 28 × 8 ins
Joseph H. Hirshorn Collection, New York *Photo : Robert E. Mates*

Mathematical model,
Science Museum, London
Crown copyright

way as the Futurists solidified the sweep of an arm or a leg. Th
result is austere, not extravagant.

Although not members of the constructivist movement, the wor
of such differing sculptors as Max Bill (b. 1908), Barbara Hep
worth (b. 1903) and Henry Moore (b. 1898) has at various time
been influenced by constructivist forms. Certain of Hepworth'
sculptures have an affinity with the mathematical solids, an
Moore used strings to trace hyperbolic parabaloids.

Max Bill has worked much like a composer of music, taking variou
themes, often mathematical series of proportions, and producin
sets of variations. One such theme has been the folded and twiste
endless loop, which produces a mathematical paradox, a solid forr
with only one traceable surface. The later works of Hepworth
Moore and Bill have not the rotational axis which plays such
large part in the work of the pure Constructivists, and are stati
by comparison.

BARBARA HEPWORTH:
Pelagos, 1946, height 16 ins
wood with colour and strings
Tate Gallery, London *By courtesy of the Trustees. Photo: Newlyn Studio*

HENRY MOORE: Bird Basket,
1939, lignum vitae and string,
length 17 ins
Private collection Photo: Lidbrooke

The classical language of sculpture came to an end when it was no longer capable of expressing the artist's ideas. Each sculptor could no longer look to his predecessors for support. The tradition of sculpture continued, but it was seen by the artist to be a tradition of being true to one's time, and of being concerned with ideas rather than with the language used to express them. The individual sculptor was on his own. He had to live his own history of art and ideas in his own lifetime.

The freeing of the concept of sculpture from a strict discipline of permitted forms led to a new appreciation of all forms of art and of all periods, both on the part of the artist and the interested layman. Printing had become both better and cheaper. No sooner were discoveries made by experimenting artists or dug up by archaeologists, than they were widely published and illustrated accurately enough to be available to all interested persons. The artist, more conscious of art history and its wide range of forms than ever before, was swamped by a flood of material to choose from in his search for a language or form of his own.

Picasso, the most eclectic of artists, quoted from all sources of form in his work, from African sculpture to cave painting, from Egyptian, Graeco-Roman and Mycenean sources, never copying but finding material that suited the purpose of the moment. If one may call this eclecticism positive, to distinguish it from a mere blind borrowing, then it also applies to the sculptor Henry Moore. The earliest influence on Moore was that of Epstein, specifically Epstein's carvings. Moore became a dedicated carver, the most important of his time, with the faith and patience essential to such a disciplined method.

Perhaps the greatest of the carver's disciplines is that he has to work under the knowledge that his output is going to be limited by the time taken by his technique, especially when the majority of his contemporaries are working much more rapidly in clay, wax and plaster, with the added advantage of being able to produce identical castings in sets. Moore was next influenced by pre-Columbian American carving, and to a lesser extent by the Constructivists. A third and very strong influence was his observation of the erosion of wind and water upon stone, from the pebbles on the beach to standing stone outcrops in the landscape. This latter source was particularly linked to his philosophy of carving, that the carver must bring out the quality of his stone, not reduce it to that anonymous state in which a piece of sculpture might just as well have been modelled and cast as carved. Moore has often chosen the most intractible wood and stone for his carvings, as if to safeguard against habit supplanting concentration and effort. His technique is the closest today to the classical technique of wearing away rather than slicing away stone. The difficulties of the medium have ensured that his various sources of discovery have been subordinated to the personal character of his sculpture.

Other sculptors to make use of quotations from the past have been Giacometti (b. 1901), with his strong references to Etruscan and Sardinian archaic bronze figures and Marino Marini (b. 1901), who has ranged from Greek and Cycladic figures to the Romanesque.

MARINO MARINI: Cavaliere, 1947, bronze, height 6.5 ins
Tate Gallery, London *By courtesy of the Trustees*

SIR JACOB EPSTEIN:
The Rock Drill, 1913–14, bronze,
27.75 × 23 × 17.5 ins
Tate Gallery, London
By courtesy of the Trustees

ALBERTO GIACOMETTI:
Man Pointing, 1947, bronze,
height 17 ins
Tate Gallery, London
By courtesy of the Trustees

HANS ARP: Forest, 1916,
painted wood relief
Roland Penrose collection, London

Another source for ideas has been that of Surrealism. When Freud
exposed men's dreams to the light of day, he showed them to be
the key to the unconscious mind. Dreams are full of pictorial
symbols; their essence is the visual pun, a form of rebus. Artists
were quick to seize on this imagery as a source in both painting and
sculpture.

Broadly speaking this might be done in two ways. First, by the
direct analogy or visual pun. The early Epstein sculpture *Rock Drill*
of 1913 is a direct rebus. The figure is robot-like, made up of
machine components, the drill itself. There is also a deliberate
resemblance to the baboon-like animal, the mandrill.

The second and rather more subtle approach is for the sculptor to
let his subconscious mind produce its own free images, without
any direct conscious literal interference. The delicate free forms
of Hans Arp (b. 1887) are in this category. Often completely non-
figurative, they are not constructions in the constructivist sense

nor absolute form in the Hepworth or Moore. Bordering on Surrealism were the anti-rational objects of Dada. The derisive label was self-attached by members of the movement as a protest against everything, including all forms of art, all modern movements. They exhibited ready-made articles with punning titles as sculpture – a urinal became *The Fountain*, a bottle rack *Tree* – these by Marcel Duchamp (b. 1887), and members derided the machine age by making machines that were purposeless, an answer to the machine-based sculptures which paid machines homage.

These movements which sought the unconscious rather than the conscious, which turned their backs on reason and logic, were the product of disillusion. Before the first World War the foundation of the modern movement was well laid and enjoyed enlightened patronage. The war was as much a shock to the avant-garde as to those who could look back comfortably to nineteenth-century ideas of progress. The war and its miseries, which continued long afterward, destroyed for many the faith in reason that the hard, well constructed, built to last looking painting and sculpture seemed to epitomise. The peace which was no real peace but rather an armed truce between the two wars, saw some consolidation of the main constructive element in the Modern Movement, but this was dealt another blow by the second World War and by the threat of a further atomic war. Violence breeds violence, and a new sculpture has been born from it. The new phase can hardly be described as a movement, for political disillusion has made artists wary of the associations which sprang up so freely in the earlier part of the century. For the most part unhappy with society, the artist has turned more than ever to his own personality, as if anything outside himself is of uncertain validity. His language can be found in all the previous phases of the Modern Movement, yet the new image tends to horror and despair.

The image is generally anthropomorphic. I use this word literally rather than figuratively, for human suffering and emotions are implied in robot-like figures assembled from the ready to hand work of mass-production and the scrap yard. Picasso had shown the way with his *Bull's Head* assembled from the handlebars and saddle of a junk yard bicycle, and with his *Ape* which has a toy motor car for a head, but the stricken figures of Eduardo Paolozzi (b. 1924), built out of the proliferation of small parts of modern technology, have an air of martyrdom about them. The figures of

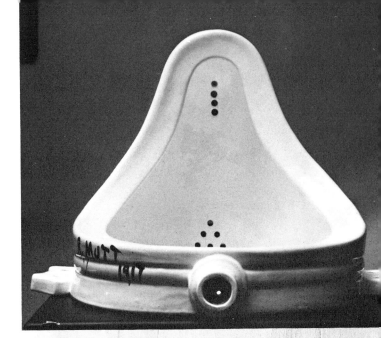

MARCEL DUCHAMP:
Fountain, signed 'R. Mutt 1917'
replica of original
which has been lost
Photo : Galleria Schwarz, Milan

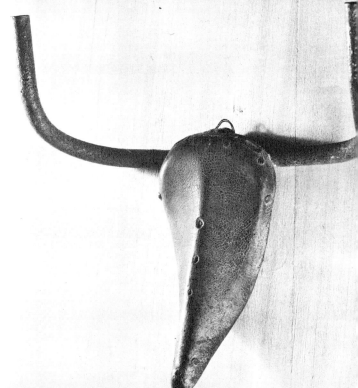

PABLO PICASSO:
The Bull (Metamorphosis), 1943,
bicycle saddle and handlebars
Collection the artist. © S.P.A.D.E.M.,
Paris 1965. *Photo : Chevojon, Paris*

Germaine Richier (1904-1959) and Ralph Brown (b. 1928) look like the mutilated victims of war returned to reproach the survivors for still being alive. Although not so menacing, the figures of Kenneth Armitage (b. 1916) and Bernard Meadows (b. 1915) have an air of awaiting impending disaster.

All the foregoing sculptors work in wax, clay or plaster, which is cast in bronze. The present period has seen a great revival of the lost wax method of bronze casting, which has also found new industrial applications.

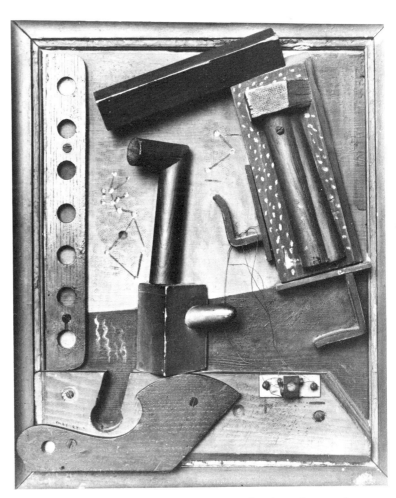

MAX ERNST: Fruit of Long Experience, 1919, painted wood on metal
Roland Penrose Collection, London *Photo: Brompton Studio*

EDUARDO PAOLOZZI:
Poem for the Trio MRT
(Marevich, Rodchenko, Tatlin),
welded aluminium, height 85 ins
width 44 ins, length 86 ins
Robert Fraser Gallery, London
photo: David Farrell

EDUARDO PAOLOZZI:
Hermaphrodite Idol no. 1, 1962
Courtesy Robert Fraser Gallery, London
Photo: David Farrell, Gloucester

KENNETH ARMITAGE: Figure lying on its side, 5th version, 1957
British Council, London *Photo: Lidbrooke*

The modelling itself often looks like an assault upon the material. The method, a rapid one, gives strong evidence of the sculptor's being in a hurry, as if there was no time to lose. The 'unfinish' which Rodin took from Michelangelo and used as a stamp of self assertion is no longer a symbol of the personal element in sculpture, but a deliberate end in itself. The work is a protest against the machine age in its finish and form. The junk-yard sculptures do not deride the machine as did the Dadaists, they accuse it of destroying the society it was to have created.

The sense of urgency, the feeling that time is short, has affected all schools of thought in sculpture. Today's Constructivists tend to use ready-made extruded sections of metals for their work, from wire on one hand to full size girder sections on the other.

The manufacture of sculpture out of ready-made objects perhaps began with the modern sculptor's return to 'nature' as a reaction against the studies of plaster casts in an antique room, a pursuit which had become custom without meaning.

BERNARD MEADOWS: Black Crab, 1953, bronze, height 17 ins
Gimpel Fils Gallery Ltd., London

GERMAINE RICHIER:
The Bat, 1952
Collection the artist. (From Sir Herbert
Read: A Concise History of Modern
Sculpture, Thames & Hudson Ltd.,
London, 1964)

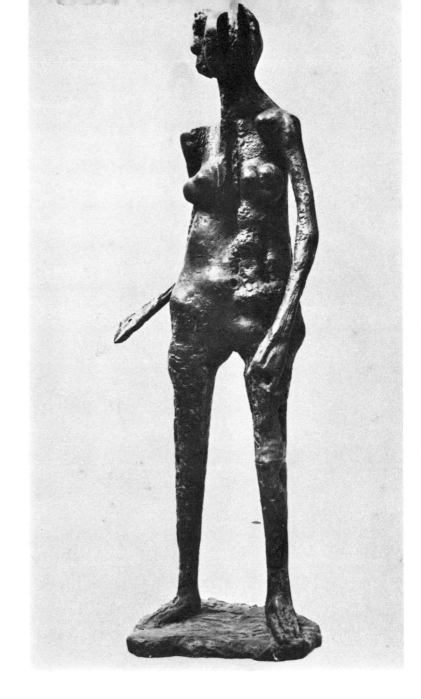

RALPH BROWN:
Turning Woman, 1962, bronze,
height 36 ins
Collection the artist

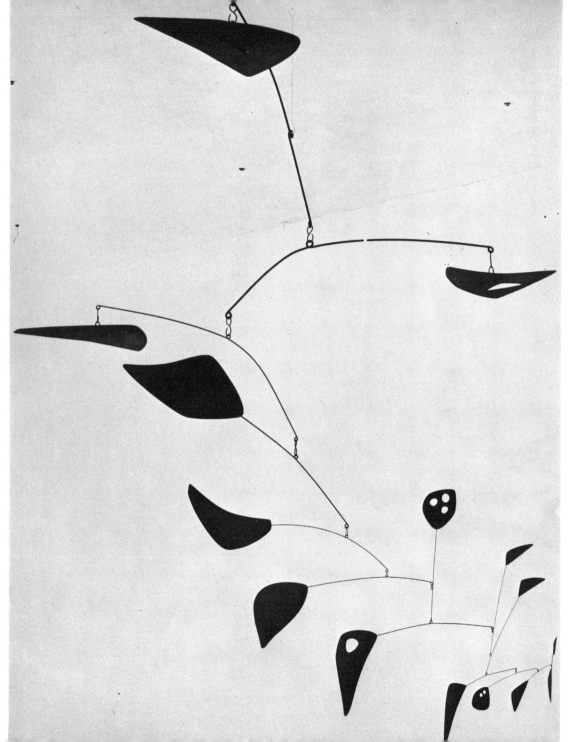

ANTHONY CARO: Lock, 1962, steel painted blue, height 34 ins, width 10 ins, length 9 ft 3 ins
Kasmin Gallery, London

At first this appreciation was limited to sea-worn pebbles and driftwood, or wind-shaped rocks. Then Picasso and Duchamp pointed out in their work that man-made objects are as much part of the world as 'natural' objects.

On the one hand sculptors search the junk heaps for the detritus of civilisation, out of which they produce figures to mock society. On the other they search the hardware catalogues for brand new castings, mouldings and extensions to cut up and assemble into sculpture

Paolozzi has produced equally disturbing figures by both methods. Alexander Calder (b. 1898) and Anthony Caro (b. 1925) produce sculptures which look like sub-assemblies in a shipyard. Louise Nevelson (b. 1900) uses the full range of wood turnery to assemble giant magic boxes of building shapes.

George Fullard's (b 1924) Cubist sculptures make use of ready-to-

ALEXANDER CALDER:
Hanging large-leaf-composition,
1954 wrought iron,
99.25 × 106.25 ins
Les Musées Municipaux d'Amsterdam

GEORGE FULLARD: The Cross of St George, 1964

HENRY MOORE: Warrior with shield, 1943–54, bronze, height 5 ft
Art Gallery, Toronto, Institute of Art, Minneapolis, Museum and Art Gallery, Birmingham,
Städtische Kunsthalle, Mannheim *Photo: Lidbrooke*

hand wood mouldings from the builder's yard. Even Henry Moore has produced fragments, archaic figures that look as if they have suffered the accidents of time. Moore has always produced a quantity of cast figures and objects, rather small in size and closely related to his current carvings. The qualities of the metals were always subordinated to finished form. His recent *Warrior* is not related to any carving. It is a figure on the defensive against over-whelming force. It is rough and blurred at the edges, unlike Moore's early preoccupation with finish and precision.

Movement is no longer elaborately implied in sculpture but has become actual. Alexander Calder first produced his mobiles in the 1930's. These are carefully balanced, branching suspensions, part surrealist, with a delicate, playful quality, rather like giant toys. The moving sculpture of today is sinister and powerful. The elaborate machines of Jean Tinguely (b. 1925) are intended to batter them-selves to pieces .With their attendant firework displays they have the aspect of a simulated air-raid.

EAN TINGUELY :
os, 1964,
eight 125 cms
alerie Iolas, Paris

Conclusion

Broadly speaking the path of modern sculpture is divided and parallel. At one extreme we have the constructivist movement concerned with non-representational forms of mathematical precision and purity, and its implicit faith in reason and logic. At the other we have the sculpture of feeling rather than thinking. Figurative or not, it seems to cry aloud, appealing for mercy rather than justice.

At these extremes the differences are clear. Between them there are no well defined boundaries. Constructivism has a strong connection with Cubism, but Cubism is still the dominant formal factor in expressionist sculpture too. The more literal form of Surrealism has waned, but both Constructivists and Expressionists are influenced by surrealist discoveries.

Carving has been mainly supplanted by modelling, casting and fabrication-welding. This is partly for economic reasons, for suitable woods and stone have become extremely expensive, and the time taken in working them is another factor in a sculptor's earnings. In the past, the sculptor worked as the leader of a team of assistants within the framework of a guild, a workshop or atelier. His techniques were derived from those of the ordinary stone mason, wood worker or metal-founder.

Today the sculptor prefers to be a solitary worker. He may be found at work pinching his forms out of wax between finger and thumb, dribbling wet plaster freely over a complex light metal armature, cutting a mould from foamed plastic blocks with a hot wire, or engrossed in choosing ready-made forms from industrial castings or metal sections, in size ranging from curtain runners to full-sized rolled steel joists.

In industrial language he will fabricate rather than cast, for he can use the welding torch for cutting and joining sheet metal single handed. Foundry work depends upon skilled assistants, is complex and expensive, and there are comparatively few founders for the sculptor to take his work to. However, the combination of materials and time has been chiefly affected by the sculptor's need for techniques that are immediate and direct, and that allow of free alteration. The carver is always working in the future until his work is finished. The modeller can more easily achieve the work of the moment, an important factor in both sculpture and painting today.

The new materials such as fibre glass and plastics have yet to be used seriously by sculptors. So far they have only been used for lightweight castings of imitation antiques, and for a few attempts at decorative reliefs, part mural and part sculpture, which hitherto have been rather eclectic and derivative.

While there will always be a need for private sculpture, from good portraiture to pure abstraction, the immediate future development will probably be environmental sculpture. Modern architecture and sculpture developed closely together in the early days of the movement. Perhaps modern architecture should be sculpture in itself, with no need of sculpture as applied decoration. In the seventeenth and eighteenth centuries the public place, whether in a park or a town, was regarded as sculpture, and this is one of the most important contributions that sculpture could make today. This would mean involving sculptors in the actual designs of buildings and cities, as the Constructivists at one time wished.

It is more difficult to try to forecast the future of the sculpture of protest. If people are constantly exposed to protest, they become accustomed to its presence and ignore it. There is always the tendency to turn one's back on unpleasantness anyway, and this is one of the reasons for such sculpture. But like satire, protest must die with its target. What survives is the form, which can remain just as powerful long after its creator's intention is forgotten. Only time can sort out the survivors here; it has always been a lucky critic who could spot a winner in his own generation. Moral problems never die, however, but are born again with each new generation for it to solve them in its own way, and it has always been an important function of the artist to act as social critic.

In the meantime sculpture generally, because of its total effect, its all or nothing quality as an art form, remains one of the most difficult of the arts to understand, and consequently one of the most powerful and rewarding.